THE BEST EVER BOOK OF BRIGHTON AND HOVE ALBION JOKES

Lots and Lots of Jokes
Specially Repurposed for You-Know-Who

Other books by Mark Young

The West Australian Joke Book
How To Promote Your Business
Dr. Young's Guide to Demotivating Employees
Guide To Selling Your Home

And about 600 other books titled:

The Best Ever Book of ...... Jokes

To find out more, check out our websites at:

www.dolyttle.com, www.thebesteverbook.com

or visit

www.amazon.com

THE BEST EVER BOOK OF BRIGHTON AND HOVE ALBION JOKES

Lots and Lots of Jokes
Specially Repurposed for You-Know-Who

Dolyttle & Seamore
New York, New York

The Best Ever Book of Jokes: Lots and Lots of Jokes Specially Repurposed for You-Know-Who

Dolyttle & Seamore
New York, New York

Dolyttle & Seamore
198 Garth Road Suite 2DD
Scarsdale, NY 10583

Publisher's Cataloging-in-Publication Data

The Best Ever Book of Jokes: Lots and Lots of Jokes Specially Repurposed for You-Know-Who.

p. cm.
ISBN-13: 9781490585239
ISBN-10:1490585230

10 9 8 7 6 5 4 3 2 1

To All Those People
Who Think They Have a Sense of Humor —But Don't

INTRODUCTION

In my world, nothing is original. While I may be the only person who believes this, it's true. I have heard almost every joke in this book at least a hundred times—the only difference is the victim— a different ethnic, racial or religious group.

I grew up in Australia where the victim was Irish. In other states and countries the victim is often Jewish, Blond, Italian, Libyan, Catholic, Mexican, Polish, Australian, Norwegian, Essex Girl, Newfie, Mother-in-Law, etc.

Just because the person being picked on varies from country to country, it doesn't mean they're a hated minority. I would argue that it means that they're loved (after all, almost everybody wants to be the center of attention). In most cases, the goal is not humiliation, because the jokes being told are not nasty—they're funny—or at least they're supposed to be.

With that said, sit down, put on your happy face and prepare to be transported back to a time when you were young and innocent, and your friends tried to put a smile on your face.

And, if you're offended, sorry, no offence is intended. Just remember that perception is everything, and the way you perceive these jokes says a lot about you.

Mark Young

Why do people take an dislike to Brighton and Hove Albion Fans?

To save time later.

———•———

Two Brighton and Hove Albion Fans were helping a friend open a new store, and decided to take a break. Since the shop wasn't due to open for a few days, the shelves were not fully set up.

One Brighton and Hove Albion Fan said to the other: "I bet some old fogey will walk by, put his or her face to the window, and ask what we're selling."

No sooner were the words out of his mouth, when an old woman peeked through the window and cheerfully asked: "What are you selling?"

"We're selling assholes," replied one of the Brighton and Hove Albion Fans sarcastically.

Without skipping a beat, the lovely old lady said: "You must be doing well. You've only got two left."

———•———

What do you call a Brighton and Hove Albion Fan who practices birth control??

A humanitarian.

Why do Brighton and Hove Albion Fans make great astronauts?

They took up space in school.

Two Brighton and Hove Albion Fans were riding their bikes across a university campus when one said: "Where did you get such a great bike?"

The second Brighton and Hove Albion Fan said: "I was walking across town yesterday, minding my own business, when a beautiful woman rode up on this bike, threw it to the ground, took off all her clothes and said: "Take what you want."

The first Brighton and Hove Albion Fan nodded approvingly and said: "Good choice; the clothes wouldn't have fit you anyway."

There was a Brighton and Hove Albion Fan who was late for work during the power failure because he got stuck on the escalator.

Two Brighton and Hove Albion Fans in a kayak were chilly, so they lit a fire in the craft. It sank, proving once again that you can't have your kayak and heat it too.

A Brighton and Hove Albion Fan was staying with a friend and asked if there was anything he could do to help out.

"Sure," said the friend. "I'd really appreciate it if you could pick up a carton of milk when you're out. If they have eggs, get six."

A couple of hours later the Brighton and Hove Albion Fan returned with six cartons of milk.

"Why did you buy six cartons of milk?," asked the friend.

"They had eggs," replied the Brighton and Hove Albion Fan.

Why did the Brighton and Hove Albion Fan cut a hole in the carpet?

To see a floor show.

Did you hear about the Brighton and Hove Albion Fan who went to a mind reader?

There was no charge.

Why don't Brighton and Hove Albion Fans eat pickles?

They can't get their head in the jar.

———•———

A Brighton and Hove Albion Fan met a fairy who said she would grant her one wish.

"I want to live forever," said the Brighton and Hove Albion Fan.

"Sorry," said the fairy. "I can't grant wishes like that!"

"Fine," said the Brighton and Hove Albion Fan. "I want to live until Congress gets its heads out of its ass!"

"Crafty bastard," said the fairy.

———•———

A Brighton and Hove Albion Fan with one ear want into a bar.

"Do you want a beer?," asked the bartender.

The Brighton and Hove Albion Fan: "I've got one ear."

———•———

Four workers were on the top floor of a high-rise building project when Steve fell off the roof and died instantly.

After the body was taken away by the ambulance, they held a meeting to decide who would tell Steve's wife that he was killed in a horrible accident.

Finally, one of the workers said: "I used to be a Brighton and Hove Albion Fan, so I'm pretty good at delivering bad news, I'll do it."

Two hours later, he came back carrying a case of beer.

"Where did you get the beer?," asked one of the workers.

"Steve's wife gave it to me," he said.

The worker replies: "That's unbelievable, you told the lady her husband was dead and she gave you the beer?"

"Well not exactly," said the Brighton and Hove Albion Fan. "When Steve's wife answered the door, I said to her: 'You must be Steve's widow.'"

She said: "No, I'm not a widow."

And I said: "I'll bet you a case of beer you are."

————

How did the Brighton and Hove Albion Fan die ice fishing?

She was run over by the Zamboni machine.

————

Hear about the Brighton and Hove Albion Fan who broke both legs ironing the curtains?

She fell out the window.

An evil genie captured a Brighton and Hove Albion Fan and her two friends and banished them to the desert for a week. The genie allowed each person to bring one thing.

The first friend brought a canteen so he wouldn't die of thirst.

The second friend brought an umbrella to keep the sun off.

The Brighton and Hove Albion Fan brought a car door, because if it got too hot she could just roll down the window!

—·—

Did you hear about the Brighton and Hove Albion Fan who broke an arm raking leaves?

Fell out of the tree"

—·—

A Brighton and Hove Albion Fan took a second job in a restaurant to earn some extra cash for the holidays. All went well until the boss said: "Please fill the salt shakers."

It took the Brighton and Hove Albion Fan three hours to put the salt through the hole in the top of the container.

—·—

Three Brighton and Hove Albion Fans took a small plane to the wilderness in northern Canada to hunt moose over a weekend. The pilot said: "Please remember that this is a very small plane. You can only bring back one moose between you."

But of course each Brighton and Hove Albion Fan killed their own moose and come Sunday, they told the pilot that last year they each brought their own moose on the plane. The pilot agreed to let them take all three dead moose home.

Just after takeoff, the plane stalled and crashed. In the wreckage, one of the Brighton and Hove Albion Fans woke up, looked around and said: "Where the hell are we."

"Oh, about a hundred yards east of the place where we crashed last year," replied one of the other Brighton and Hove Albion Fans.

———•———

Did you hear about the Brighton and Hove Albion Fan who lost $50 on a baseball game?

He lost another $50 on the replay.

———•———

What do you call a Brighton and Hove Albion Fan on a Harley wearing a leather jacket?

A rebel without a clue.

———•———

A crooked Brighton and Hove Albion Fan and two other prisoners escaped from jail. They ran into the woods and all hid in the trees.

When the guard shined his flashlight up the tree, the first prisoner said "meow." The guard said: "It's just a cat."

When the guard shined his flashlight up the next tree, the prisoner said: "whooo, whooo." The guard said: "It's just an owl."

When he shined his flashlight up the third tree, the Brighton and Hove Albion Fan said: "Moo, moo."

———•———

How many Brighton and Hove Albion Fan jokes are there?

None, they're all facts.

———•———

A Brighton and Hove Albion Fan was asked to be the Groomsman at a friend's wedding, but had to refuse because he didn't know anything about horses.

———•———

A Brighton and Hove Albion Fan was being honored by his peers at an award dinner, when suddenly there was a flash of light and God appeared before the Brighton and Hove Albion Fan.

God, turned to the Brighton and Hove Albion Fan and said:

"You have made a great contribution to your field and I would like to reward you for everything you've done. You have the choice of infinite wealth, boundless wisdom or utter beauty. Pick one."

Without hesitating, the Brighton and Hove Albion Fan said: "Wisdom."

"Done!," said God, and disappeared in a cloud of smoke and a bolt of lightning.

There was a great silence as everyone looked at the Brighton and Hove Albion Fan. Finally, a voice called out: "Say something wise."

The Brighton and Hove Albion Fan turned to the crowd and said: "I should have taken the money."

——•——

There was a Brighton and Hove Albion Fan who sent 10 puns to friends, hoping that at least one of the puns would make them laugh. No pun in ten did.

——•——

How do you make a Brighton and Hove Albion Fan laugh on Monday morning?

Tell her a joke on Friday night.

——•——

Three Brighton and Hove Albion Fans driving from Boston to

Disneyland.

After three days they arrived at their destination and turned around and went home after they saw the sign saying: "Disneyland left."

———•———

A Brighton and Hove Albion Fan was taken to the hospital after suffering a heart attack. While on the operating table, the Brighton and Hove Albion Fan had a near death experience. Seeing God, she asked: "Is my time up?"

God said: "No, you have another 15 years, 2 months and 8 days to live."

Upon recovery, the Brighton and Hove Albion Fan decided to get a face lift, liposuction and a tummy tuck.

Upon release from hospital, the Brighton and Hove Albion Fan crossed the street, was killed by a bus.

Arriving in heaven the Brighton and Hove Albion Fan screamed at God: "You said I had another 15 years? Why didn't you pull me from out of the bus's path?"

God replied: "I'm sorry, I didn't recognize you."

———•———

A Brighton and Hove Albion Fan was driving down I-95 when her cell phone rang. Her friend said: "Be careful, there's a car going the wrong way on I-95."

The Brighton and Hove Albion Fan replied: "They got it wrong, it's not one car, it's hundreds of them!"

———•———

Do you know how to save a drowning Brighton and Hove Albion Fan?

No?... Good!

———•———

A Brighton and Hove Albion Fan was walking down the street with a paper bag. He ran into one of his friends who asked what was in the bag. The Brighton and Hove Albion Fan said: "Fish."

The friend said if I can guess how many fish you have in the bag, you'll have to give me one."

The Brighton and Hove Albion Fan said: "I'll tell you what, if you can tell me how many fish I have, I'll give you both of them."

———•———

Why won't a shark attack a Brighton and Hove Albion Fan swimming in the ocean?

Professional courtesy.

———•———

A Brighton and Hove Albion Fan received a parrot as a gift. The parrot had a bad attitude and an even worse vocabulary. Every word out of the bird's mouth was rude, obnoxious and laced with profanity.

The Brighton and Hove Albion Fan tried to change the bird's attitude by saying only polite words, playing soft music and doing anything possible to "clean up" the bird's vocabulary.

Finally, the Brighton and Hove Albion Fan was fed up and yelled at the parrot. The parrot yelled back. The Brighton and Hove Albion Fan shook the parrot, and the parrot got angrier and angrier and ruder and ruder. In desperation, the Brighton and Hove Albion Fan grabbed the bird and put him in the freezer.

For a few minutes the parrot squawked and kicked and screamed. Then suddenly there was total quiet. Not a peep was heard for over a minute. Fearing that he'd hurt the parrot, the Brighton and Hove Albion Fan opened the door to the freezer.

The parrot calmly stepped out into the Brighton and Hove Albion Fan's arms and said: "I believe I may have offended you with my rude language and actions. I'm sincerely remorseful for my inappropriate transgressions and I fully intend to do everything I can to correct my rude and unforgivable behavior."

The Brighton and Hove Albion Fan was stunned at the change in the bird's attitude.

As the Brighton and Hove Albion Fan was about to ask the parrot why he had made such a dramatic change in his behavior, the bird said: "May I ask what the turkey did?"

Where can you find a good Brighton and Hove Albion Fan?

In the cemetery.

Did you hear about the Brighton and Hove Albion Fan who froze to death outside a theater?

He was waiting to see the movie "Closed for the Winter."

A Brighton and Hove Albion Fan went out bear hunting and spotted one in the bushes and blasted away. The Brighton and Hove Albion Fan investigated but couldn't find the bear. As he was about to give up, he felt tap tap on his shoulder and when he turned around saw the bear.

The bear said: "You know, it's not bear hunting season?"

The Brighton and Hove Albion Fan answered: "Yes, I know."

The bear took the rifle and smashed it on a rock, threw the hunter across a tree trunk, pulls his pants down and gave it to him. He then told the Brighton and Hove Albion Fan: "Get out of here. I don't want to see you again."

The Brighton and Hove Albion Fan was incensed, so he raced back to town and bought the biggest bear rifle he could find, and returned to the forest. A few minutes later, he spotted the bear and emptied his rifle. He then searched for the body, but couldn't find it.

He then felt a tap on his shoulder, and surprise, surprise, it was the bear again.

"I thought I told you not to come back," said the bear. The bear then proceeded to smash the new rifle, and again threw the Brighton and Hove Albion Fan to the ground and gave it to him again. "This is the last time I'm warning you. Don't come back."

The Brighton and Hove Albion Fan went berserk. When he got back to town, he bought a M16 and went straight back to the forest. Thinking he saw the bear in a bush, he took aim and emptied the entire M16. Still no body, until, a familiar tap on the shoulder.

"You're not in this for the hunting, are you?," asks the bear.

———•———

Friend: "Please close the window. It's cold outside."

Brighton and Hove Albion Fan: "If I close the window, will it get warm outside?"

———•———

How did the Brighton and Hove Albion Fan die while drinking milk?

The cow fell on her.

———•———

A Brighton and Hove Albion Fan was worried that his wife was losing her hearing and he thought she might need a hearing aid. Not quite sure what to do, he called the family doctor to discuss the problem.

The doctor suggested a simple informal test that he could perform to test his wife's hearing loss. "Stand about 40 feet away from your wife," said the doctor, "and in a normal speaking voice ask her a question. If she doesn't respond, go to 30 feet, then 20 feet, and so on until you get a response."

That evening, the Brighton and Hove Albion Fan's wife was in the kitchen cooking dinner, and he was watching TV in the family room. He said: "I'm about 40 feet away, let's see what happens."

In a normal tone he asks: 'Honey, what's for dinner?" No response. So the Brighton and Hove Albion Fan moved closer to the kitchen, and repeated the question.

Still no response.

He then went into the dining room, about 20 feet from his wife and asked the question a third time. Again no response.

He then walked up to the kitchen door, about 10 feet away from his wife and loudly repeated the question. Still nothing.

Finally he walks up to her and says: "Honey, what's for dinner?"

"For the fifth time, we're having spaghetti," said the wife.

———•———

How do you sink a Brighton and Hove Albion Fan's submarine?

Knock on the hatch.

A Brighton and Hove Albion Fan from Montreal sent his photo to a lonely hearts club.

They wrote back saying they weren't that lonely.

A Brighton and Hove Albion Fan is at the post office buying stamps for her holiday cards.

"May I have 50 Chanukah stamps and 50 Christmas stamps?, said the Brighton and Hove Albion Fan."

The clerk asked: "What denomination?"

"Oh my god!," the woman exclaimed. "Has it really come to this? Give me 16 Orthodox, 22 Conservative and 12 Reform Chanukah cards, and 20 Catholic, 18 Greek Orthodox and 12 Lutheran Christmas stamps."

A Brighton and Hove Albion Fan was refused service in a restaurant. "We don't serve Brighton and Hove Albion Fans here," said the waiter.

That's OK said the Brighton and Hove Albion Fan, I don't eat Brighton and Hove Albion Fans."

How can you confuse a Brighton and Hove Albion Fan?

You can't. They're born that way.

After being married for 44 years, a Brighton and Hove Albion Fan took a careful look at his wife one day and said: "Darling, 44 years ago we had a cheap apartment, a junky car, slept on a sofa bed and watched a 10-inch black and white TV. But I got to sleep with a hot 21-year-old girl every night. Now I have a million dollar home, a $60,000 car, a big bed and a large-screen TV, but I'm living with a 65-year-old woman. It seems to me that you're not holding up your side of things."

The Brighton and Hove Albion Fan's wife replied: "No problem. If that's what you want, go for it. If you want to sleep with a 21-year-old, I'll make sure you once again get to live a cheap apartment, drive a junky car, sleep on a sofa bed and watch a 10-inch black-and-white TV!"

Did you hear about the man who wanted to be buried at sea?

His Brighton and Hove Albion Fan died trying to dig the grave

---

Why did the Brighton and Hove Albion Fan write TGIF on his shoes?

To remind him that Toes Go In First.

If you see a Brighton and Hove Albion Fan on a bicycle, why

shouldn't you hit him?

He might be riding your bicycle.

A Brighton and Hove Albion Fan and his wife were sitting around the breakfast table one lazy Sunday morning. The Brighton and Hove Albion Fan turned to his wife and said: "When I die, I want you to sell all my stuff."

"Why would you want me to do that?," asked his wife.

"I figure that you'll eventually remarry, and I don't want some asshole using my stuff," replied the Brighton and Hove Albion Fan.

The Brighton and Hove Albion Fan's spouse said: "What makes you think I'd marry another asshole?"

A police officer pulled over a Brighton and Hove Albion Fan and asked to see his license.

The Brighton and Hove Albion Fan said: "I wish you would make up your mind. Yesterday when you pulled me over you took away my license—now you want me to show it to you."

Why did God make snakes just before Brighton and Hove Albion Fans?

Practice.

A man walked into a bar with his alligator and asked the bar tender if they served Brighton and Hove Albion Fans.

"Sure do," replied the bar tender.

"Great," said the man. "Give me a beer, and I'll have a Brighton and Hove Albion Fan for my alligator."

There was a Brighton and Hove Albion Fan flying in a helicopter to a town 50 miles away. Suddenly everything went black.

After they crashed the pilot said: "What happened?"

The Brighton and Hove Albion Fan said: "I got cold, so I turned off the fan."

Ship's captain: "Please divert your course 15 degrees to the north to avoid a collision."

Brighton and Hove Albion Fan: "Recommend you divert your course 15 degrees to the south to avoid a collision."

Ship's captain: "This is the captain of a US Navy ship. I say again, divert your course."

Brighton and Hove Albion Fan: "No. I say again, you divert your course."

Ship's captain: "This is the aircraft carrier USS Lincoln, the second largest ship in the United States Atlantic fleet. We are accompanied by three destroyers, three cruisers and numerous support vessels. I demand that you change your course 15 degrees north. That's one-five degrees north, or counter measures will be undertaken to ensure the safety of this ship."

Brighton and Hove Albion Fan: "I'm a Brighton and Hove Albion Fan on vacation with my family in a lighthouse. Your call."

———•———

What's the difference between a Brighton and Hove Albion Fan and a bucket of dirt?

The bucket.

———•———

A Brighton and Hove Albion Fan and a friend were sitting in a bar, drinking beer.

The Brighton and Hove Albion Fan turned to his friend and said: "I'm tired of going through life being a drain on society. Tomorrow, I'm going to go down to the college and enroll in a class that will help me make society a better place."

The next day, the Brighton and Hove Albion Fan goes down to the college, meets the admissions officer and enrolls in a course called Logic.

At the first class, the lecturer explains that logic helps you to figure out how the world works. To demonstrate, he calls the Brighton and Hove Albion Fan up to the front of the classroom.

The lecturer asks: "Do you own a weed eater?"

"Yes," replies the Brighton and Hove Albion Fan.

"Then logically speaking, I could reasonably conclude that you have a yard," said the lecturer.

"True," said the Brighton and Hove Albion Fan, "I do have a yard."

The lecturer went on. "Because you have a yard, I think that you also have a house."

"That's right," said the Brighton and Hove Albion Fan.

"And, because you have a house, there's also a good chance that you have a family."

"Right again," said the Brighton and Hove Albion Fan. "I have a family."

"I'm not done," said the lecturer. "Because you have a family, then logically you must have a wife. And, because you have a wife, logic tells me you must be a heterosexual."

"I am a heterosexual," replied the Brighton and Hove Albion Fan. "I'm impressed that you were able to work out so much about me without me having to say a word—just because I own a weed eater."

A couple of weeks later, the Brighton and Hove Albion Fan and his friend are again drinking. He tells his friend that he's studying logic, and offers to demonstrate his new-found knowledge.

The Brighton and Hove Albion Fan asks his friend: "Do you own a weed eater?"

"No," replied the friend.

"Then you're gay," proclaimed the Brighton and Hove Albion Fan.

———•———

Did you hear about the terrorists who hijacked a plane full of Brighton and Hove Albion Fans?

They threatened to release one each hour until their demands were met.

———•———

There was a Brighton and Hove Albion Fan who waited two hours at the side door of a movie theatre to see the stars come out.

———•———

A Brighton and Hove Albion Fan was watching the scuba divers jump off a boat when his friend turned to him and said: "Why do the scuba divers always fall backwards off the boats?"

The Brighton and Hove Albion Fan replied: "Because if they fell forwards they'd still be in the boat, wouldn't they?"

———•———

Four Brighton and Hove Albion Fans were on a plane to Las Vegas for a conference when the first Brighton and Hove Albion Fan said: "We've all worked together for many years, but don't really know one another. I suggest we tell each other something about ourselves that nobody knows.

They look nervously at each other, but nod OK. The first Brighton and Hove Albion Fan says: "Since I suggested it, I'll go first. With me it's alcohol. Every so often, I go down to a bar and drink myself silly for a few days. Not only can't I remember what I did, I have to make up an excuse to explain my absence."

They all look each other nervously, but the next Brighton and Hove Albion Fan slowly starts: "With me, it's gambling. Periodically,
I go down to the casino and spend a couple of months salary, and then have to explain to my wife what happened. Not easy."

The third Brighton and Hove Albion Fan, who is really nervous, reluctantly says: "This is very difficult. With me it's women. Every so often I go down to the red light district, pick out a girl, and spend a week in the saddle. I really have problems explaining where I've been to my wife."

They all look at the fourth Brighton and Hove Albion Fan, waiting. He doesn't say anything. Then one of the four speaks up: "Come now, we've all told our innermost faults. It's your turn."

He looks at the others and starts hesitantly.

"Well," he says, "I'm an inveterate gossip, and I can't wait to get off this plane."

How do you confuse a Brighton and Hove Albion Fan?

Place three shovels against a wall and ask him to take his pick.

———·———

What is the difference between a Brighton and Hove Albion Fan and a pothole?

People don't run over the same pothole more than once.

———·———

A couple recently celebrated their 50th wedding anniversary and invited their three sons, all very successful Brighton and Hove Albion Fans, to a dinner that was being hosted by their local community to celebrate this momentous occasion.

The first son arrived 30 minutes late and said: "Happy anniversary. Sorry I'm late, but there was a lot of traffic on the freeway and I didn't have time to get you a gift."

"Not to worry," said the father. "The important thing is that we're together today."

Son number two arrived 45 minutes late and announced: "Happy anniversary. You and mom look great. I had a last minute meeting with a client, and I only just made my plane. Sorry, but I didn't have time to shop for you."

"Don't even think about it," said the father, "we're glad you were able to come."

Five minutes later their youngest son arrived from across town and said: "Hello and happy anniversary! I'm sorry, but my boss made me work today and I was so busy packing for my vacation, I didn't have time to get you anything."

"It's fine," said the father, "at least we're all here."

After they had finished dessert, and the members of the community had dispersed, the father turned to his three Brighton and Hove Albion Fan children and said: "There's something your mother and I have wanted to tell you for a long time.

"When we were young, we were very poor. Despite this, we were able to send each of you to college. Throughout the years your mother and I knew that we loved each other very much, but we just never found the time to get married."

The three children gasped and son number two said: "You mean we're all bastards?"

"Yes," said the father.

"And cheap ones too."

———•———

Why did the Brighton and Hove Albion Fan cut a hole in his umbrella?

So he could see when it stopped raining.

———•———

Why don't they give Brighton and Hove Albion Fans coffee breaks?

It takes too long to retrain them.

Two Brighton and Hove Albion Fans went out one night and got very drunk. Thinking it wasn't a good idea to drive, they decided to walk. After a few minutes, one Brighton and Hove Albion Fan said: "I'm tired and drunk, I'm never going to make it home."

Since they had no money for a cab, they kept walking until they hit the bus terminal. The two Brighton and Hove Albion Fans looked at each other and one said: "Why don't we steal a bus?"

"Good idea," said the other.

One Brighton and Hove Albion Fan stood guard, and the other went inside to steal a bus. After 15 minutes, the Brighton and Hove Albion Fan yells: "What's happening? Haven't you found a bus yet."

The other Brighton and Hove Albion Fan screams back: "I can't find a 52."

"No problem," replies the other. "Just grab a 75 and we'll walk from the traffic lights."

A Brighton and Hove Albion Fan was telling his friend why his rent had gone up. "I told the landlord that I wanted to live in a more expensive apartment, so he raised my rent."

Why do Brighton and Hove Albion Fans wear slip-on shoes?

You need an IQ of at least 4 to tie a shoelace.

———•———

A Brighton and Hove Albion Fan was lost wandering around the desert when he came across a clothing store. Desperate for a drink, he went inside and asked the owner if he could have a glass of water.

"I'm sorry," said the store owner, "you're in the middle of the desert, I don't have any water —but I could sell you a nice tie."

"I don't need a tie," screamed the Brighton and Hove Albion Fan. "I need a glass of water."

Maintaining his composure, the storeowner said: "I'm sorry that I don't have any water, but over that big hill is a restaurant where you'll be able to buy food, water or any type of drink you want."

The Brighton and Hove Albion Fan left cursing and started walking toward the hill.

An hour later, the totally dehydrated Brighton and Hove Albion Fan returned. "I'd like to buy a tie please," he said.

"What made you change your mind," asked the storeowner.

"Your brother wouldn't let me into his restaurant without a tie."

———•———

A Brighton and Hove Albion Fan goes to his doctor and asks

for the result of the tests.

"I have bad news and worse news," says the doctor.

"Oh, what's the bad news?," asks the Brighton and Hove Albion Fan.

The doctor replies: "You only have 24 hours to live."

"That's terrible," said the Brighton and Hove Albion Fan. "How could the news possibly get any worse?"

The doctor replies: "I've been trying to call you since yesterday!"

—·—

What's the difference between a Brighton and Hove Albion Fan and a gigolo?

A gigolo only screws one person at a time.

—·—

A short balding Brighton and Hove Albion Fan is sitting at the bar staring at his drink when a large, trouble-making biker steps up next to him, grabs his drink and gulps it down in one swig.

"Whatcha gonna do about it?," asks the biker menacingly, as the Brighton and Hove Albion Fan bursts into tears.

"Come on," says the biker. "I didn't think you'd cry. I can't stand to see a man crying."

"This is the worst day of my life," said the Brighton and Hove Albion Fan.

"I'm a complete failure. I was late to a meeting and my boss fired me. Then I went to the parking lot and discovered that my car had been stolen and that my insurance had expired. I hailed a cab, forgot my wallet on the back seat and went home. When I got there, I found my wife in bed with another guy and my dog attacked me.

"Feeling depressed, I came to this bar to work up the courage to end it all. I bought a drink, dropped the suicide capsule in it, and sat here trying to get the nerve to swallow it, when you showed up and grabbed the drink out of my hands.

"I can't even commit suicide. It's just not my day."

———•———

A Brighton and Hove Albion Fan walks into the bakery and buys a cherry pie.

"Would you like it cut into four pieces or eight pieces?," asked the salesgirl.

"Better make that four pieces," said the Brighton and Hove Albion Fan. "I'm on a diet."

———•———

A waiter comes over to a table full of Brighton and Hove Albion Fans and asks, "Is anything all right?

———•———

A Brighton and Hove Albion Fan owned a small ranch in Montana. The Montana Department of Labor claimed he wasn't paying his employees properly and sent an agent out to interview him.

"I need a list of your employees and the documentation showing how much you pay them," demanded the agent.

"No problem," replied the Brighton and Hove Albion Fan. "I have a farm hand who's been with me for three years. He earns $700 a week for 40 hours, plus free room and board.

"Then there's the cook. She's worked for me for 18 months. I pay her $550 per week for 40 hours, plus free room and board.

"Then there's the half-wit," said the Brighton and Hove Albion Fan. "He works at least 18 hours every day, and does 90% of the work. He makes around $50 per week and pays for his own room and board. When times are good, he gets a free bottle of bourbon on Saturday night.

"I want to meet the half-wit," says the agent.

"Pleased to make your acquaintance," replied the Brighton and Hove Albion Fan.

———•———

What's a definition of disappointment?

A busload of Brighton and Hove Albion Fans going off the edge of a cliff—with one empty seat.

———•———

One winter morning a Brighton and Hove Albion Fan and her husband were listening to the radio during breakfast.

The announcer came on and said: "We're expecting 8- to 10-inches of snow today. Park your car on the even-numbered side of the street, so the snowplows can get through."

Not wanting to get a ticket, the Brighton and Hove Albion Fan went outside and moved the car to the even-numbered side of the road.

A week later, the announcer said: "It's a miserable winter. We're expecting another 10- to 12-inches of snow today. Park your car on the odd-numbered side of the street, so the snowplows can get through."

The Brighton and Hove Albion Fan went out and moved her car to the odd-numbered side of the street.

The same thing happened a couple of days later when they were having breakfast, but before they could hear which side of the street to park the car, the power went out.

"What do we do now?," said the Brighton and Hove Albion Fan. "I have no idea where to park the car."

The husband said: "Why don't you just leave it in the garage?"

———•———

A Brighton and Hove Albion Fan was drinking with a few friends. After the bar closed, a drunk Brighton and Hove Albion Fan brought a few of his friends back to his new apartment so they could keep the party going for a couple of hours.

He took them into the living room where there was a big brass gong and a mallet.

"What's that brass gong?," one of the guests asked.

"It's not a gong, it's a talking clock," the Brighton and Hove Albion Fan replied.

"No way," replied his astonished friend.

"Yup," replied the drunk Brighton and Hove Albion Fan.

"How's it work?," the friend asked.

"Watch," the drunk Brighton and Hove Albion Fan replied. He picked up the mallet, gave it an ear-shattering pound and stepped back.

The three friends stood looking at one another, when all of a sudden someone on the other side of the wall screamed: "You asshole! It's 3:15 in the morning!"

———•———

What do you call a Brighton and Hove Albion Fan with half a brain?

Gifted.

———•———

An elderly Brighton and Hove Albion Fan and his wife were having dinner at another couple's house. After eating, the wives left the table and went into the kitchen to get some coffee for the men.

The two gentlemen were talking, and the Brighton and Hove

Albion Fan said: "Last night we went to a new restaurant and it was really great. I recommend it very highly."

The other man said: "What's the name of the restaurant?"

The Brighton and Hove Albion Fan thought and thought and finally said: "What is the name of the flower you give to someone you love? You know, it's red and has thorns."

"You mean a rose?," asked the friend

"Yes," said the Brighton and Hove Albion Fan. He then yelled: "Rose, what's the name of the restaurant we went to last night?"

———•———

Why did the Brighton and Hove Albion Fan climb over the glass wall?

To see what was on the other side.

———•———

During a recent password audit, it was found that a Brighton and Hove Albion Fan was using the following password:

MickeyMinniePlutoHueyLouieDeweyDonaldGoofySacramento

When they asked the Brighton and Hove Albion Fan why she needed such a long password, she said she was told that it had to be eight characters long and include at least one capital.

———•———

How do you keep a Brighton and Hove Albion Fan busy for hours?

Write "please turn over" on both sides of a piece of paper.

———•———

How do you drive a Brighton and Hove Albion Fan crazy?

Give him a bag of M&Ms and tell him to alphabetize them.

———•———

A Brighton and Hove Albion Fan was walking to the deli along with two of his employees when he tripped over a bottle.

The Brighton and Hove Albion Fan picked the bottle up, rubbed the sides and a genie appeared. The genie offered each of them one wish.

"I wish I was on a beach in a tropical island," said the first employee. Immediately her wish was granted.

"I wish I was on a tour of France," said the second employee. Immediately his wish too, was granted.

It was now time for the Brighton and Hove Albion Fan to make his wish.

"I want my employees back in their offices right after lunch," moaned the Brighton and Hove Albion Fan.

———•———

What do Brighton and Hove Albion Fans use for birth control?

Their personalities.

A circus owner ran an ad for a lion tamer and two people showed up. One was a Brighton and Hove Albion Fan and the other a blonde in her mid-twenties.

The circus owner tells them: "I'm not going to sugar coat it. This is one ferocious lion. He ate my last tamer so you guys better be good or you're history. Here's your equipment—a chair, whip and a gun. Who wants to try out first?"

The girl says: "I'll go first." She walks right past the chair, the whip and the gun and steps right into the lion's cage. The lion starts to snarl and pant and begins to charge her. About half way there, she throws open her coat revealing her beautiful naked body. The lion stops dead in his tracks, sheepishly crawls up to her and starts licking her feet and ankles. He continues to lick and kiss her entire body for several minutes and then rests his head on her feet.

The circus owner's mouth is on the floor. He says: "I've never seen a display like that in my life." He then turns to the Brighton and Hove Albion Fan and asks: "Can you top that?"

The Brighton and Hove Albion Fan replies: "No problem, just get that lion out of the way."

A Brighton and Hove Albion Fan was sitting in a bar having a drink and watching the 10 o'clock news. There was a story about a man on a ledge of a building preparing to jump came on. The Brighton and Hove Albion Fan turns to the customer next to him asked: "Do you think he'll jump?"

The customer says: "I bet he'll jump."

The Brighton and Hove Albion Fan says: "I bet you $20 he won't."

Just as the customer placed her money on the bar, the guy jumped off of the building, falling to his death.

The Brighton and Hove Albion Fan handed his $20 to the customer and said: "All's fair. Here's your money."

The customer replies: "I can't take your money. I saw the 6 o'clock news and knew he'd jump."

"So did I," said the Brighton and Hove Albion Fan, "but I didn't think he'd do it again."

———•———

Did you hear about the Brighton and Hove Albion Fan who locked his keys in his car?

He needed a coat hanger to get his family out.

———•———

Three friends went down to Mexico one night, got drunk, and woke up in jail, only to find that they were to be executed in the morning. Unfortunately, none of them could remember what they did the night before.

The first friend was strapped in the electric chair, and was asked if she had any last words.

She said: "I believe in the almighty power of God to intervene on the behalf of the innocent." The prison warden threw the switch and nothing happened.

Immediately, the prison warden begs her for forgiveness, and sets her free.

The second friend is strapped in and says: "I am a law student and I believe in the power of justice to intervene on the part of the innocent." They threw the switch again, nothing happened.

The prison warden begs her for forgiveness, and releases her.

The last one, a Brighton and Hove Albion Fan, is strapped in and says: "Before I became a Brighton and Hove Albion Fan, I was an electrician, and I can tell you right now, you're not going to electrocute anybody if you don't plug this thing in."

———•———

A Brighton and Hove Albion Fan was on a United flight to Australia and the flight attendant asked him if he wanted any dinner.

"What are my choices?," asked the Brighton and Hove Albion Fan.

"Yes or no," replied the flight attendant.

———•———

What's the difference between a Brighton and Hove Albion Fan and a
vulture?

Vultures wait until you're dead to rip your heart out.

The Brighton and Hove Albion Fan was sitting in a fine restaurant with his wife when she looked over at a nearby table and saw a man in a drunken stupor.

The Brighton and Hove Albion Fan said: "You've been watching that man for some time now. Do you know him?"

"Yes," replied the wife. "He's my ex-husband. He's been drinking like that since I left him seven years ago."

"That's amazing," the Brighton and Hove Albion Fan replies, "I didn't think anybody could celebrate for that long."

Did you hear about the lion walking through the woods eating deer droppings?

He had just eaten a Brighton and Hove Albion Fan and was trying to get the taste out of his mouth!

A Brighton and Hove Albion Fan walked into a bar and ordered martini after martini, each time removing the olives and placing them in a jar.

When the jar was filled with olives, the Brighton and Hove Albion Fan got up to leave.

"Excuse me," said a customer, who was puzzled over what the

Brighton and Hove Albion Fan had done. "Why did you put all the olives from your drinks in the jar?"

The Brighton and Hove Albion Fan replied: "My wife just sent me out for a jar of olives!"

———•———

What do Brighton and Hove Albion Fans and sperm have in common?

A sperm has one-in-3 million chance of actually becoming a human being.

———•———

Three friends were stumbling home from a bar one night and found themselves on the road which led past the old cemetery.

"Come have a look over here," said one friend. "It's Michael Rosenbaum's grave. He lived to the ripe old age of 87."

"That's nothing," said the second friend. "Here's one named Patrick Bradley, it says here that he was 95 when he died."

Just then, the Brighton and Hove Albion Fan yells out: "Good God, here's a guy who lived to be 145!"

"What was his name?," asks friend number two.

The Brighton and Hove Albion Fan stumbles, and awkwardly lights a match to see what else is written on the stone marker, and exclaims: "It's Miles, from Dallas."

———•———

How do you get a Brighton and Hove Albion Fan to laugh at a joke on Saturday?

Tell it to him on Wednesday.

———•———

A Brighton and Hove Albion Fan needed a vacation and decided that ice fishing was what he needed to relieve his tension.

After arriving at his destination a couple of days later, he started to drill, when all of a sudden he heard a loud booming voice yelling: "There's no fish down there."

He stopped, moved over a few feet and started drilling for a second time. Again, he heard the loud booming voice yelling: "There's no fish down there."

So the Brighton and Hove Albion Fan moved over about 50 feet and started to drill for the third time. The same loud booming voice again broke the silence and said: "There's no fish there either."

Getting nervous, the Brighton and Hove Albion Fan looked around, saw nobody and asked: "Who are you? God?"

"No," replied the booming voice. "I'm the ice skating arena manager."

———•———

What do you call 25 skydiving Brighton and Hove Albion Fans?

Skeet.

A Brighton and Hove Albion Fan and his friend were both patients in a mental hospital. One day, while they were walking around the hospital's swimming pool, his friend jumped into the pool and promptly sank to the bottom.

Thinking quickly, the Brighton and Hove Albion Fan jumped in and pulled his friend out.

When the medical director heard about the Brighton and Hove Albion Fan's heroic act, he immediately ordered him released as he was considered mentally stable.

When he went to tell the Brighton and Hove Albion Fan the news he said: "I have good news and bad news. The good news is you're being discharged, as you were able to rationally respond to a crisis by jumping in and saving your friend's life.

"The bad news is that your friend hung himself in the bathroom with his bathrobe belt right after you saved him."

The Brighton and Hove Albion Fan said: "He didn't hang himself, I hung him there to dry. How soon can I go home?"

What's the difference between a dead skunk on the road and a dead Brighton and Hove Albion Fan on the road?

Vultures will eat the skunk.

A Brighton and Hove Albion Fan walks into a bar. The

bartender
asks: "What will you have?"

The Brighton and Hove Albion Fan says: "Give me three pints of beer, please."

So the bartender brings him three pints and the man proceeds to alternately sip one, then the other, then the third until they're gone. He then orders three more.

The bartender says: "I know you like them cold. You don't have to order three at a time. I can keep an eye on it, and when you're low, bring you a fresh cold one."

"You don't understand," said the Brighton and Hove Albion Fan. "I have two brothers, one in Dallas and one in Nevada. We made a vow to each other that every Saturday night we'd still drink together. So right now, each of my brothers has three beers, and we're drinking together."

The bartender thought that was a wonderful tradition.

Every week the man came in and ordered three beers. Then one week he came in and ordered only two. He drank them and then ordered two more.

"I know your tradition," said the bartender. "And I'd just like to let you know that I'm sorry one of your brothers died."

"My brothers are fine," said the Brighton and Hove Albion Fan. "I only ordered two beers because I've quit drinking."

—•—

A Brighton and Hove Albion Fan was working on a construction site to earn extra cash. The boss needed a wheelbarrow. A short time later the Brighton and Hove Albion Fan returned with two wheelbarrows, one on top of another.

The boss said: "I only wanted one."

The Brighton and Hove Albion Fan said: "What did you want me to do, carry it?"

———•———

A Brighton and Hove Albion Fan was flying to New York in a four-engine plane, when the pilot announced that one engine had failed and there would be a 30-minute delay. The pilot said there was no reason for concern as the jet had three more engines. The same announcement was made two more times.

Finally, the Brighton and Hove Albion Fan turned to the person in the next seat and said: "I hope the other engine doesn't fail, or we'll be up here all day."

———•———

What's the difference between a Brighton and Hove Albion Fan and a trampoline?

You take off your shoes before you jump on a trampoline.

———•———

A Brighton and Hove Albion Fan was touring Europe in a chauffeur-driven Mercedes-Benz. The Brighton and Hove Albion Fan asked the driver what the emblem on the front of the car was for.

The driver said it was to line up parking inspectors. Nothing else was said until they saw a parking inspector writing tickets.

The Brighton and Hove Albion Fan asked the driver to demonstrate the device. The driver carefully lined up the parking inspector and went straight for him—swerving at the last minute.

Suddenly there was a loud bang. "What happened?," asked the driver.

"The Brighton and Hove Albion Fan said: "You would have missed him if I hadn't opened the door."

———•———

An elderly Brighton and Hove Albion Fan is hit by a car and brought to the hospital.

The nurse asks: "Are you comfortable, sir?"

The Brighton and Hove Albion Fan replied: "I make a living."

———•———

A Brighton and Hove Albion Fan hired a plumber to do a couple of jobs around his house. When he received the bill he was angry to find he had been charged $350 an hour.

The Brighton and Hove Albion Fan said: "I'm a highly paid professional and I don't earn that much.

The plumber said: "Neither did I when I was a professional. "

Did you hear the sad story about the Brighton and Hove Albion Fan who was given a pill that was supposed to radically increase a person's IQ. When it was given to rats, they were able to run a maze with one eye closed in half the time it took the other rats to complete the course.

Needless to say, the doctors were anxious to try it out on humans. When approval was granted, they gave it to several people including a Brighton and Hove Albion Fan, who took it faithfully every day.

Two years later, the Brighton and Hove Albion Fan earned a degree in brain surgery—an all time record.

Unfortunately, the Brighton and Hove Albion Fan was part of the control group that had been given a placebo. There he was, dumb as ever, and stuck with an advanced medical degree. What a waste. Really sad.

A Brighton and Hove Albion Fan was sitting at a bar when he notices a lamp on the bookshelf. He wanders over and begins to rub it.

Out pops a genie and offers him three wishes. Immediately he says I want a glass of beer that automatically refills itself.

A glass of beer appears. The Brighton and Hove Albion Fan drinks it quickly, and it immediately refills itself. He does the same thing two more times.

The genie then asks what he wants for his other two wishes.

Without thinking, the Brighton and Hove Albion Fan says quickly: "I'll take another two of these."

———•———

Two Brighton and Hove Albion Fans were driving to their new jobs in Florida, when they saw a sign which said "Clean bathrooms."

By the time they had reached Florida, they had cleaned 32 bathrooms.

———•———

A Brighton and Hove Albion Fan and another person applied for a part-time job waitressing to earn some extra money. Being a high-class establishment, the owner of the bar gave them both a 10 question test to determine who should get the job.

Both applicants handed in the test, and they both correctly answered the first nine questions.

The bar owner then went up to the Brighton and Hove Albion Fan and said: "You both got question 10 wrong, but based on the way you answered the question, I've decided to hire the other person.

"What do you mean?," said the Brighton and Hove Albion Fan. "How could one wrong answer be better than another wrong answer?"

"Simple," replied the bar owner. "On question 10, the other applicant wrote: 'I don't know,' and you wrote 'neither do I.'"

———•———

What is the first thing you should do if you find a Brighton and Hove Albion Fan buried up to his neck in cement?

Get more cement.

———•———

A young, Brighton and Hove Albion Fan was walking around a field in Long Island, when he came across an old lamp. He rubbed the lamp and suddenly a genie appeared before him.

"For freeing me, I will grant you one wish," said the genie.

"I wish that there was a bridge from New York to London so I don't get ripped off every time I go on vacation," said the Brighton and Hove Albion Fan.

"I'm sorry, but I can't do that," said the genie. "It would be too much change. Thousands of people would be put out of work. Government revenue would be reduced dramatically. It would mess up too many people's lives."

So the Brighton and Hove Albion Fan thought for a second and said: "OK, then. I'm a Brighton and Hove Albion Fan, and I'm tired of everyone making fun of me. I wish that Brighton and Hove Albion Fans were as smart, or smarter than everyone else in the world."

The genie said: "Would you like two lanes, or four?"

———•———

Three Brighton and Hove Albion Fans were waiting to be interviewed for a job. The first Brighton and Hove Albion Fan was called into the office, and after the normal questions was told that he would have to answer a question that tested his verbal skills.

The interviewer said: "I would like you to make a sentence using the word 'sweater.'"

The Brighton and Hove Albion Fan said: "My mother knitted me a sweater."

"I'll get back to you," said the interviewer. "Please ask the next applicant to come in."

After the second Brighton and Hove Albion Fan's interview he also was asked make a sentence using the word "sweater."

The second Brighton and Hove Albion Fan said: "My mother knitted me a sweater."

Of course, the interviewer was suspicious, but he told the Brighton and Hove Albion Fan that he would get back to him.

Getting wise, the interviewer changed the question for the third Brighton and Hove Albion Fan. Instead of asking him to use the word "sweater," he asked him to use "fascinate."

The Brighton and Hove Albion Fan said: "My mother knitted me a nice sweater with 10 buttons, but I can only fasten eight."

———•———

How can you tell if a Brighton and Hove Albion Fan is lying?

His lips are moving.

———•———

A Brighton and Hove Albion Fan returned home one night when he came across a dead body on his lawn. Thinking quickly, he called 911 and reported the incident.

"Where's the body," asked the 911 operator.

"It's at the end of Eucalyptus Drive," the Brighton and Hove Albion Fan replied.

"Could you please spell that for me?," the operator asked.

After a long pause, the Brighton and Hove Albion Fan said: "How about I drag the body over to Oak Street and you pick it up there?"

———•———

What's the difference between a Brighton and Hove Albion Fan and a vampire?

A vampire only sucks blood at night.

———•———

A Brighton and Hove Albion Fan was walking down the street with a case of beer under his arm when his friend Peter stopped him and asked what he got the case of beer for.

"I got it for my partner," replied the Brighton and Hove Albion Fan.

"Good trade," replied Peter.

———•———

A Brighton and Hove Albion Fan and two of his friends walked into a bar and ordered three beers.

Just as they were about to take a drink, three flies appeared and jumped into each glass.

The first friend pushed away the beer in disgust. The second friend scooped the fly out of the beer and started drinking as if nothing had happened.

The Brighton and Hove Albion Fan picked the fly out of his drink and started shaking it over his drink and began yelling: "Spit it out. Come on already, spit it out."

What's black and brown and looks good on a Brighton and Hove Albion Fan?

A Doberman pinscher.

What's the difference between a dead skunk on the road and a dead Brighton and Hove Albion Fan on the road?

Skid marks in front of the skunk.

You are in a room with a mass murderer, a terrorist and a Brighton and Hove Albion Fan.

You have a gun with only two bullets.

What do you do?

Shoot the Brighton and Hove Albion Fan twice.

A Brighton and Hove Albion Fan dies and goes to hell. The devil greets him warmly at the gates, and as they enter a long corridor, the devil explains that the Brighton and Hove Albion Fan must choose a room where he will spend eternity.

As they approach the first room, the door opens, and the Brighton and Hove Albion Fan peers in. There's an endless circle of people standing on hot coals with weights strapped to their backs.

"I don't think I want to spend eternity here," said the Brighton and Hove Albion Fan.

The devil then showed the Brighton and Hove Albion Fan the second room.

In this room, the damned walk around on broken glass listening to elevator music.

"This isn't much fun," said the Brighton and Hove Albion Fan. "I definitely don't want to spend any more time in this room."

In the last room, the Brighton and Hove Albion Fan was surprised to find the damned standing around up to their armpits in vomit drinking coffee.

"That doesn't look so bad!," said the Brighton and Hove Albion Fan. "I'll stay here."

"Very well," said the Devil, closing the door behind him.

"Suddenly, the room supervisor called out on his megaphone: "Alright everybody, coffee break's over. Back on your heads."

What do you call 100 Brighton and Hove Albion Fans at the bottom of the ocean?

A good start.

Santa Claus, the tooth fairy, an honest Brighton and Hove Albion Fan and an old drunk are walking down the street together when they simultaneously spot a hundred dollar bill.

Who gets it?

The old drunk, of course. The other three are mythical creatures.

How do you save a drowning Brighton and Hove Albion Fan?

Throw him a rock.

A rich man who was very close to his money got together with his Brighton and Hove Albion Fan and two of his friends. He then announced and that he was dying and had less than a month to live.

He handed each person an envelope with $100,000 in it and asked everyone to do him a favor after he died.

"Each of these envelopes contains $100,000," said the rich man. "Since I don't want to go to the afterlife without my money, would you please throw these envelopes into my coffin after I die?"

Every one in the group agreed, and took the envelopes.

About a month later, the rich man died and the group reconvened at the funeral.

As promised, each man threw his envelope into the coffin before it was closed up.

As they were leaving, the first friend said: "I have a confession to make. My local church needed a new altar, so I took $5,000 out of the envelope and bought it."

The next friend looked at his feet and said: "Since we're coming clean, I thought it was a waste of money to bury all of the money in the coffin, so I took $30,000 out of the envelope and bought the hospital a new X-ray machine.

Both men then looked at the Brighton and Hove Albion Fan, expecting him to also make a confession. "You guys are crooks," said the Brighton and Hove Albion Fan. "I didn't take any money. I put a check in the coffin for the entire $100,000."

———•———

A Brighton and Hove Albion Fan rang United and asked how long it took to fly from New York to Chicago.

"Just a minute, sir," said the United reservations clerk.

"Thank you," said the Brighton and Hove Albion Fan and hung up.

———•———

A man walked into a bar and asked the barman if he had heard the latest Brighton and Hove Albion Fan joke.

"I'm warning you," said the Brighton and Hove Albion Fan loudly, "I'm a Brighton and Hove Albion Fan who's just working part-time as a Brighton and Hove Albion Fan to make some extra money."

"That's all right," said the man. "I'll tell it slowly."

———•———

A man hired an unemployed Brighton and Hove Albion Fan as his office assistant. On the first day the phone rang, and the Brighton and Hove Albion Fan hung up immediately.

"Who was that?," asked the boss.

"Some fool saying it was long distance from Brazil," replied the Brighton and Hove Albion Fan. "I told him everybody knew that."

———•———

What's the difference between a Brighton and Hove Albion Fan and an onion?

People cry when they cut up an onion.

———•———

How do you get a Brighton and Hove Albion Fan out of a tree?

Cut the rope.

Why do Brighton and Hove Albion Fans always carry garbage in their pockets?

Identification.

A Brighton and Hove Albion Fan attended a show where a ventriloquist who fancied himself as a comedian told 20 Brighton and Hove Albion Fan jokes in a row.

"Look," shouted the Brighton and Hove Albion Fan, standing up in the audience. "I'm fed up being insulted by all these jokes. Brighton and Hove Albion Fans are not as stupid as you make out."

"Sit down," said the ventriloquist. "They're only jokes. Don't tell me that Brighton and Hove Albion Fans haven't got a sense of humor."

"Be quiet," said the Brighton and Hove Albion Fan. "I'm not talking to you. "I'm talking to the little fellow on your knee."

A man walks into a bar and says: "I hear Brighton and Hove Albion Fans are a bunch of hard drinkers. I'll bet $500 to anybody who can drink 20 glasses of whisky back-to-back."

The room is quiet, and no one takes up the man's bet. One person leaves.

Thirty minutes later the person who left returns, and taps the man on the shoulder: "Is your bet still on?," asks the Brighton and Hove Albion Fan.

"Yes," says the man and as he asks the Brighton and Hove Albion Fan to line up 20 glasses of whisky. Immediately the Brighton and Hove Albion Fan tears into all 20 glasses, and drinks them back-to-back.

The other pub patrons cheer as the man hands over the $500 to Brighton and Hove Albion Fan and says: "Why did you leave the bar before, instead of taking up my challenge when I offered it?"

The Brighton and Hove Albion Fan said: "$500 is a lot of money, so I went to the bar down the street to see if I could do it first."

———————

What do you call a Brighton and Hove Albion Fan sitting on the grass?

Fertilizer.

———————

A priest died and went to heaven. When he got there, he found a Brighton and Hove Albion Fan in line in front of him at the Pearly Gates. Saint Peter came over and said to the priest: "Just a minute, I'll be right back," as he took the Brighton and Hove Albion Fan away to his room.

A few minutes later he returned and said to the priest: "Follow me to your new quarters."

Along the way, they passed many people in their heavenly abodes, including the Brighton and Hove Albion Fan's quarters.

The priest was awe-struck by the opulence and splendor of

the Brighton and Hove Albion Fan's quarters. There were fine silks, rare foods and drinks, soft music, and attractive young women to serve him for eternity.

The priest finally arrived at his new quarters—a small 6-foot by 9-foot room with bare walls, a plain bed and a Bible for entertainment. The priest said: "I don't want to sound ungrateful, but how come the Brighton and Hove Albion Fan gets a magnificent room and I get this dump."

Saint Peter smiled and said: "We have a lot of priests here in heaven, but only one Brighton and Hove Albion Fan."

———•———

Did you hear about the Brighton and Hove Albion Fan who spent four days in Macy's looking for wheels for a miscarriage?

———•———

A Brighton and Hove Albion Fan and his friend were repairing a barn roof, when suddenly a strong wind blew and knocked their ladder down. Since there was no help nearby, both men decided to jump.

Looking around for something that would break their fall, they saw a pile of manure. The Brighton and Hove Albion Fan jumped first.

"Are you alright?," asked his friend.

"How deep is it?"

The Brighton and Hove Albion Fan answers: "I'm fine. It's only up to my knees."

"Great. Here I come," yelled the friend as he lands in a pile of manure up to his neck.

You said it was only up to your knees," cried the friend.

"It did only come up to my knees," said the Brighton and Hove Albion Fan. "I jumped head first."

———•———

Hear the one about the deaf Brighton and Hove Albion Fan?

Neither did he.

———•———

One day a Brighton and Hove Albion Fan was sitting on a beach when he saw a young woman swimming far out to sea. As he watched, he saw a shark circling her. Immediately, he jumped into the water, karate chopped the shark, killed it instantly, and helped the young woman swim to the beach.

After he got back to the beach, a journalist ran up to him and said: "That was the most courageous thing I've ever seen. I'm going to let the world know about this. You'll be famous. I can see the headline now: 'Man Saves Girl From Killer Shark.'"

"What do you do for a living?"

"I'm a Brighton and Hove Albion Fan," he replied.

"Great," said the journalist. "You'll see the story in tomorrow's paper."

The next day, the Brighton and Hove Albion Fan bought the paper and the headline read: "Brighton and Hove Albion Fan Kills Girl's Pet."

———•———

A young Brighton and Hove Albion Fan decided to turn his life over to God and thought that the best way to do this was to become a monk, so he checked himself into a monastery.

At his indoctrination the head monk told him that they were sworn to TOTAL silence—but every 10 years they were permitted to speak two words.

After 10 years of total silence, the head monk indicated it was now time for the former Brighton and Hove Albion Fan to speak his two words.

The monk said: "Bed hard," and then resumed his silent study and work.

Another 10 years passed, and the head monk again indicated it was time for him to speak his two words.

The monk said: "Food bad," and the former Brighton and Hove Albion Fan then resumed his silent study and work.

Thirty years after entering the monastery, it was again time for the former Brighton and Hove Albion Fan to speak, this time he said: "I quit."

The head monk shook his head and said: "I knew this was coming. You've done nothing but complain for the past 30 years!"

———•———

Did you hear about the Brighton and Hove Albion Fan who was asked to be a Jehovah's Witness?

He refused because he didn't see the accident.

———•———

A Brighton and Hove Albion Fan went to his doctor and said he had a serious problem because he could never remember what he said.

"When did you first notice this problem?," asked the doctor.

"What problem?," asked the Brighton and Hove Albion Fan.

———•———

A Brighton and Hove Albion Fan was jumping up and down on the floor yelling and screaming when a friend walked into the room.

"What's wrong?," asked the friend.

"Nothing, nothing at all," relied the Brighton and Hove Albion Fan. "I'm just so happy. I finished a jigsaw puzzle in record time."

"How long did it take you?, asked the friend."

"Six months," replied the Brighton and Hove Albion Fan. "On the box it said three to five years."

———•———

Not all Brighton and Hove Albion Fans are bad, but it's a crying shame that the other ninety-nine percent make the rest look bad.

———•———

A drunk climbs on a bar stool in a bar and screams: "All Brighton and Hove Albion Fans are thieves."

A man stands up and says: "I resent that remark."

The drunk shouts back: "Are you a Brighton and Hove Albion Fan?" "No," says the man "I'm a thief."

———•———

A Brighton and Hove Albion Fan and his wife in their 60s were visited by a fairy who granted them both a wish.

"I want to travel round the world with my darling husband," said the Brighton and Hove Albion Fan's wife.

Two tickets for a luxury cruise magically appeared in her hand.

A couple of minutes later the Brighton and Hove Albion Fan said: "Sorry, but my wish is to have a wife 30 years younger than me."

The fairy waved her wand, and suddenly he was 92.

———•———

Did you hear about the Brighton and Hove Albion Fans' Rubik's cube?

It's white on all sides and it takes two seconds to solve.

A Brighton and Hove Albion Fan went to a pet shop and asked how many budgie birds were in stock. "We have 99 birds," replied the shop owner. "I'll take them all," said the Brighton and Hove Albion Fan. He went to a tailor and had 99 pockets sewn into his jacket. He then put a budgie bird in each pocket and went up to the top of the tallest building in town and jumped off.

The Brighton and Hove Albion Fan hit the ground with an almighty smack and lay there groaning until a person passed by and asked him what had happened. "I don't know," replied the Brighton and Hove Albion Fan. "But that's the last time I try budgie jumping."

Two Brighton and Hove Albion Fans were walking home one night after drinking when a severed head rolled along the ground in front of them.

The first Brighton and Hove Albion Fan picked it up, and asked if it was their good friend Mike. "No," said the second Brighton and Hove Albion Fan: "Mike was taller than that."

An unemployed Brighton and Hove Albion Fan got a job at a sawmill. Just before lunch, he yelled: "Dave, I lost my finger."

"How did you do it?," asked Dave.

"I just touched this big spinning thing here, like thi…," replied the Brighton and Hove Albion Fan.

"Darn! There goes another one!," yelled the Brighton and Hove Albion Fan.

—•—

How do you brainwash a Brighton and Hove Albion Fan?

Give him an enema.

—•—

A Brighton and Hove Albion Fan opened her morning newspaper and was dumbfounded to read in the obituary column that her best friend Susan had died. Before she could do anything, the phone rang. It was Susan.

"Did you see my obituary in today's newspaper?," asked Susan. "It said I died!!"

"Of course I saw it," replied the Brighton and Hove Albion Fan. "Where are you calling from?"

—•—

What do you have when a Brighton and Hove Albion Fan is buried up to his neck in sand?

Not enough sand.

—•—

A Brighton and Hove Albion Fan was staggering home after

a hard night of drinking with a bottle of wine in his back pocket when he slipped and fell badly. Struggling to his feet, the Brighton and Hove Albion Fan felt something wet running down his leg.

"Please, God," implored the Brighton and Hove Albion Fan, "let it be blood!"

A Brighton and Hove Albion Fan went to trial for armed robbery when the jury foreman came out and announced: "Not guilty."

"That's great," shouted the Brighton and Hove Albion Fan.

"Does that mean I can keep the money?," the Brighton and Hove Albion Fan asked the judge.

What does a Brighton and Hove Albion Fan say when you blow in his ear?

"Thanks for the refill!"

A Brighton and Hove Albion Fan phoned the maternity ward. "Quick," he said. "Send an ambulance, my wife is having a baby!"

"Tell me, is this her first baby?," the doctor asked.

"No, this is her husband Kevin," replied the Brighton and Hove Albion Fan.

A Brighton and Hove Albion Fan and his friend were catching the subway late one night when they came across a notice stating: "Dogs Must Be Carried On the Escalator."

"Great," said the Brighton and Hove Albion Fan to his friend. "Where am I going to find a dog at this time of night?"

———•———

Two mothers were bragging about their sons.

The first said: "My son is such a saint. He studied hard, got himself a degree, doesn't smoke, and he hasn't so much as looked at a woman in over two years."

The Brighton and Hove Albion Fan's mother responds: "My son is also quite a saint. He studied hard, became a Brighton and Hove Albion Fan and not only hasn't he not looked at a woman in more than three years, but he hasn't touched any liquor in all that time."

"My word," said the first mother. "You must be so proud."

"I am," said the Brighton and Hove Albion Fan's mother. "And, when he gets out of jail, I'm going to throw him a huge party."

———•———

Brighton and Hove Albion Fan: "My dog fell down a hole and I had to shoot it."

Friend: "Did you shoot it in the hole?"

Brighton and Hove Albion Fan: "No, in the head."

———•———

A Brighton and Hove Albion Fan, wanting to earn some money, decided to hire herself out as a handyman and started canvassing a wealthy neighborhood.

She went to the front door of the first house and asked the owner if he had any jobs for her to do.

"Well, you can paint my porch," replied the homeowner. "How much will you charge?"

The Brighton and Hove Albion Fan said, "How about $50?"

The homeowner agreed and told her that the paint and ladders were in the garage.

The homeowner's wife heard the conversation and asked her husband: "Does she realize that the porch goes all the way around the house?"

"She should," said the homeowner. "She was on the porch."

A short time later, the Brighton and Hove Albion Fan came to the door to collect her money.

"You're finished already?," the homeowner asked.

"Yes," the Brighton and Hove Albion Fan answered. "Since I had some paint left over, I decided to give it two coats."

Impressed, the homeowner reached in his pocket for the $50.

"And by the way," the Brighton and Hove Albion Fan added, "It's not a Porch, it's a Ferrari."

What do you call a Brighton and Hove Albion Fan with two brain cells?

Pregnant.

———•———

Two Brighton and Hove Albion Fans won $5,000,000 in a lottery. While having a drink one night, the first Brighton and Hove Albion Fan said to the second Brighton and Hove Albion Fan:

"What are we going to do about the begging letters?"

The second Brighton and Hove Albion Fan said:

"We're going to continue sending them out?"

———•———

Hear about the Brighton and Hove Albion Fan who got stuck in a bear trap?

Chewed off both arms and one leg and still couldn't get away.

———•———

A broke Brighton and Hove Albion Fan decides to ask God for help.

"Dear Lord," he prays. "If I don't get some cash, I'm going to lose everything. Please let me win the lottery."

Lottery night comes, but the Brighton and Hove Albion Fan doesn't win.

He prays even harder, saying: "God, why have you forsaken me? My children are starving. Please just let me win."

Suddenly there is a blinding flash of light, and the Brighton and Hove Albion Fan hears God speak.

"Work with me on this," God says. "Buy a ticket."

———•———

How do you keep a Brighton and Hove Albion Fan happy in his old age?

Tell him jokes when he's young.

———•———

A Brighton and Hove Albion Fan walks into a doctor's office and tells the doctor she's broken every single bone in her body.

"That's impossible," says the doctor.

The Brighton and Hove Albion Fan says: "It's true. Look!" She then touches her leg with her index finger and screams: "Ouch!"

Then she touches her arm and yells: "Eeeeoooow!"

Finally she touches her ribs and can barely maintain her composure as the tears start to roll down her face.

"See, I told you I broke every bone in my body," she said.

The doctor rubs his chin, then conducts a thorough examination.

"Well, Miss," he tells her, "I've got some good news and some bad news. The good news is, you haven't broken every bone in your body. The bad news is, you've broken your finger."

———•———

An executive was interviewing a Brighton and Hove Albion Fan for a position in his company. He wanted to find out something about her personality so he asked: "If you could have a conversation with someone, living or dead, who would it be?"

The Brighton and Hove Albion Fan quickly responded, "The living one."

———•———

How do you tell the Brighton and Hove Albion Fan on an oil drilling platform?

He's the one throwing bread to the helicopters.

———•———

Did you hear about the Brighton and Hove Albion Fan who took a roll of toilet paper to a crap game?

———•———

"So, have you figured what to buy your wife for the holidays?," asked Sam.

"I sure have," replied the Brighton and Hove Albion Fan.

"My wife made it easy. She said she wanted something with diamonds, so I bought her a deck of cards."

A Brighton and Hove Albion Fan returned home from work early one day and found his wife in bed with another man.

Upset, he grabbed his gun and pointed it at his head, which made his wife burst out laughing.

"What are you laughing at," cried the Brighton and Hove Albion Fan. "You're next.

How many Brighton and Hove Albion Fans does it take to screw in a light bulb?

How many can you afford?

An unemployed Brighton and Hove Albion Fan and his wife moved to a farm to reduce costs and work out what to do while the economy recovered. Their modest house had no running water or electricity.

Nine months after they moved, the Brighton and Hove Albion Fan's wife's water broke and the doctor arrived.

"What do you want me to do, doctor?," asked the Brighton and Hove Albion Fan.

"Hold the lantern. Here it comes," said the doctor as he held up child for all to see.

"Congratulations, you're the proud father of a ...," said the doctor.

Before he could finish his sentence, the doctor said: "Wait a minute. Hold the lantern," and the doctor delivered a beautiful baby daughter to the Brighton and Hove Albion Fan and his wife.

A couple of minutes later he again shouted: "Hold the lantern," and moments later held up a third baby.

"Doctor," asks the Brighton and Hove Albion Fan, "Do you think it's the light that's attracting them?"

———•———

A cop pulls over two Brighton and Hove Albion Fans who were very drunk.

He says to the first: "What is your name and address?"

The Brighton and Hove Albion Fan replies: "I'm Mark Johnstone of no fixed address."

The cop turns to the second Brighton and Hove Albion Fan, and asks the same question.

"I'm David Harris, and I live in the apartment above Mark."

———•———

A drunk Brighton and Hove Albion Fan gets on a bus and asks the conductor how long the trip is between New York and Boston.

"About four hours, depending on traffic," said the driver.

"Okay," says the drunk. "How long is the trip between Boston and New York?"

The bus driver says to the Brighton and Hove Albion Fan: "It's still about four hours. Why do you think there'd be a difference?"

"Well," says the drunk Brighton and Hove Albion Fan: "It's only a week between Christmas and New Year, but it's a lot longer between New Year and Christmas!"

———•———

How do you save a drowning Brighton and Hove Albion Fan?

Take your foot off his head.

———•———

Why did the Brighton and Hove Albion Fan put dynamite in his trunk?

In case he needed to blow up his tires.

———•———

A Brighton and Hove Albion Fan and his two friends were about to go down the waterslide when a wrinkled old man steps in front of them.

"This is a magic ride," says the wrinkled old man. "You will land in whatever you shout out on the way down."

"I'm game," said the first friend and shouted "Gold," at the top of his voice as he slid down the slide. When he hit the bottom he found himself surrounded by thousands of gold coins.

The next friend shouted "Silver" at the top of her voice, and landed in more silver coinage than she knew what to do with.

The Brighton and Hove Albion Fan went last and, launching himself from the top of the slide shouted "weeee!"

———•———

Why do they bury Brighton and Hove Albion Fans 20 feet deep after they die?

Because deep down they are really nice people.

———•———

How do you get a Brighton and Hove Albion Fan to climb on the roof of a bar?

Tell him drinks are on the house!

———•———

A Brighton and Hove Albion Fan lived with his dog for many years, and when the dog died, he went to his local parish priest and asked if services could be said for his dog.

The priest said: "No, we can't have services for a dog here, but that new church down the street that might be willing to do it."

"Thank you," said the Brighton and Hove Albion Fan. "Do you think $50,000 is a big enough donation?"

"Why didn't you tell me the dog was Catholic?," said the priest.

———•———

What's the difference between Brighton and Hove Albion Fans and pigs?

Pigs don't turn into Brighton and Hove Albion Fans when they drink.

———•———

A Brighton and Hove Albion Fan had just finished reading a book titled, You Can Be The Man of Your House."

He stormed into the kitchen and said to his wife: "From now on, you need to know that I am the man of this house and my word is law. You will prepare me a gourmet meal tonight, and when I'm done eating, you'll serve me a scrumptious dessert.

And, after dinner, you're going to go upstairs with me and we will have the kind of sex that I want. "Then, you're going to draw me a bath, wash my back and towel me dry and bring me my robe. Then, you'll massage my feet and hands. Then tomorrow, guess who's going to dress me and comb my hair?"

The Brighton and Hove Albion Fan's wife replied: "The funeral director?"

———•———

What's the difference between a Brighton and Hove Albion Fan and a computer?

You only have to punch information into a computer once.

Did you hear about the Brighton and Hove Albion Fan who studied all night for his blood test.

Why do Brighton and Hove Albion Fans hate M&Ms?

They're too hard to peel.

What do you call a Brighton and Hove Albion Fan who scores well in an IQ test?

A cheat.

There was a Brighton and Hove Albion Fan who worked hard all his life and saved all of his money, refusing to part with any of it except for essentials.

On his deathbed, the Brighton and Hove Albion Fan turned to his wife and said: "When I die, I want you to take all my money and put it in the casket with me so I take it to afterlife with me."

His wife faithfully promised to carry out his last wish and agreed to put all of his money into the casket with him.

At the funeral, the service was held and just before they closed the casket, his wife shouted: "Wait a moment, and quickly put a metal box in the casket next to the Brighton and Hove Albion Fan. The undertaker closed the casket down and rolled it away.

The wife's friend turned to her and said: "Girl, I knew you weren't foolish enough to put all of his money in the coffin, what was in the box?"

The Brighton and Hove Albion Fan's wife replied: I promised to put his money in the casket and I can't go back on my word.

"You mean to tell say, you me you put all of his money in the coffin?," said the friend.

"You bet I did," said the Brighton and Hove Albion Fan's wife. "I withdrew all his money from his bank account, put it in my checking account and wrote him a check. If he can cash it, then he can spend it."

———•———

A Brighton and Hove Albion Fan is someone who thinks the three major political parties are Republican, Democratic and Cocktail.

———•———

A Brighton and Hove Albion Fan walks into the bar and says to the bar tender: "I'll bet you $200 I can pee into that glass on the top shelf without spilling a drop."

The Brighton and Hove Albion Fan contemplates this and says: "OK."

So the Brighton and Hove Albion Fan drops his pants and pees all over the bar. When he's finished the only dry spot left is the top shelf.

The bar tender is beside himself with laughter, but stops laughing when he sees the Brighton and Hove Albion Fan laughing his head off.

"Why are you laughing?," he asks the Brighton and Hove Albion Fan, "You've just lost $200."

"Yes," said the Brighton and Hove Albion Fan. "I did lose $200, but I bet the guys outside $1,000 that I could pee all over your bar and you'd be laughing."

————•————

Why do Brighton and Hove Albion Fans drive BMWs?

Because they can't spell Porsche.

————•————

A Brighton and Hove Albion Fan boards a plane to New York with a ticket for the economy section. She looks at the seats in economy and then looks into the front cabin at the first-class seats.

Seeing that the first-class seats are larger and more comfortable, the Brighton and Hove Albion Fan takes the last empty one.

The flight attendant checks her ticket and asks the Brighton and Hove Albion Fan to move back to her seat in economy.

The Brighton and Hove Albion Fan refuses.

Flustered, the flight attendant goes to the cockpit and informs the captain of the problem.

The captain goes back and tells the woman that her assigned seat is in economy.

The Brighton and Hove Albion Fan again refuses to move.

The captain doesn't want to cause a commotion, and so he returns to the cockpit to discuss the problem with the copilot.

The copilot says that his girlfriend is a Brighton and Hove Albion Fan, and that he can take care of the problem.

He then goes back and briefly whispers something in the Brighton and Hove Albion Fan's ear.

She immediately gets up, says: "Thank you so much," hugs the copilot, and rushes back to her seat in economy.

The pilot and flight attendant, who were watching with rapt attention, together ask the copilot what he had said to the Brighton and Hove Albion Fan.

He replies, "I just told her that the first class section wasn't going to New York."

———•———

What do you call a fly in a Brighton and Hove Albion Fan's head?

Space invader.

———•———

A man gets a call from his Brighton and Hove Albion Fan

friend.

"I've got a problem," says the Brighton and Hove Albion Fan.

"What's the matter?," asks the friend.

"Well, I've bought this jigsaw puzzle, but it's too hard. None of the pieces fit together and I can't find any edges," said the Brighton and Hove Albion Fan.

"What's the picture of?," asks the friend.

"It's of a big rooster," replies the Brighton and Hove Albion Fan.

"All right," says the friend. "I'll come over and have a look."

As he gets to the Brighton and Hove Albion Fan's house, he goes into the kitchen and finds the pieces on the kitchen table.

The friend looks at the jigsaw and then turns to the Brighton and Hove Albion Fan and says: "For Pete's sake—put the cornflakes back in the box."

———•———

Why do Brighton and Hove Albion Fans' lunchboxes have clear lids?

So they can tell if it's morning or afternoon.

———•———

A Brighton and Hove Albion Fan goes to Australia for a vacation. There he meets an Aussie farmer and gets talking.

The Aussie shows off his wheat field and the Brighton and Hove Albion Fan says: "Oh! We have wheat fields that are twice as large."

Then they walk around the farm and the Aussie shows off his herd of cattle.

The Brighton and Hove Albion Fan immediately says: "We have longhorns that are at least twice as large as your cows."

The conversation has almost died when the Brighton and Hove Albion Fan sees a herd of kangaroos hopping through the field.

The Brighton and Hove Albion Fan asks: "And what are those?"

The Aussie gives the Brighton and Hove Albion Fan an incredulous look and asks: "Don't you have any grasshoppers where you come from?"

What's the difference between yoghurt and a Brighton and Hove Albion Fan?

Yoghurt has a little culture.

What's a Brighton and Hove Albion Fan's idea of safe sex?

Locking the car doors.

Did you hear about the Brighton and Hove Albion Fan who saw a notice reading: "Man wanted for Robbery and Murder?"

He went in and applied for the job.

One night a police officer saw a Brighton and Hove Albion Fan looking for something under a street light. He asked him if he had lost something there.

The Brighton and Hove Albion Fan said: "I lost my keys in the alley."

"Why are you looking under the light," asked the police officer.

The Brighton and Hove Albion Fan said: "It's a lot easier to look over here."

The circus owner puts an ad in the newspaper for a part-time, trainee lion tamer.

A Brighton and Hove Albion Fan thinks it's an easy way to make some extra money, so he applies and gets the job.

"What do I do?," asks the Brighton and Hove Albion Fan.

"Simply hold the chair, the lion will obey," said the circus owner.

"And what should I do if the lion doesn't obey?," asked the Brighton and Hove Albion Fan.

"Crack the whip," said the circus owner."

"And if that doesn't work?," asked the Brighton and Hove Albion Fan.

"You have a revolver. Shoot it into the air," said the circus owner."

"And if that doesn't work, what do I do then?," asked the Brighton and Hove Albion Fan.

"Well then, throw shit at the lion," said the circus owner who was growing tired on this line of questioning."

"Where do I get that from?," asked the Brighton and Hove Albion Fan.

"Trust me on that," said the circus owner. "You'll have plenty!"

———·———

Have you heard about the Brighton and Hove Albion Fan who cheated Amtrak?

He bought a round-trip ticket to Washington and didn't go back.

———·———

An out-of-work Brighton and Hove Albion Fan was given the job of painting the lines down the middle of a highway. On his first day, he painted six miles; the next day three miles; the following day less than a mile.

The boss came up to him and said: "Your productivity is dropping rapidly. If you don't pick up your game, I'm going to have to let you go."

The Brighton and Hove Albion Fan replied: "I just can't do any better. Each day I keep getting farther away from the paint can."

———•———

What's the difference between a puppy and Brighton and Hove Albion Fan?

If you put a puppy in a room by itself for an hour, it'll eventually stop whining.

———•———

A man died and was taken to his place of eternal torment by the devil. As he passed sulfurous pits and shrieking sinners, he saw a man he recognized as his Brighton and Hove Albion Fan snuggling up to a beautiful woman.

"That's unfair!," he cried. "I have to roast forever, and my Brighton and Hove Albion Fan gets to spend his afterlife with a beautiful woman."

"Shut up!," barked the devil, jabbing him with his pitchfork. "Who are you to question that woman's punishment?"

———•———

What's wrong with Brighton and Hove Albion Fan jokes?

Brighton and Hove Albion Fans don't think they're funny, and nobody else thinks they're jokes.

———•———

What is the difference between a catfish and a Brighton and Hove Albion Fan?

One is a scum sucking bottom dweller and the other is a fish.

———•———

Two Brighton and Hove Albion Fans went into a bar and ordered two drinks. They pulled out their lunch from their briefcases and started to eat.

The waiter became quite concerned and marched over and said: "You can't eat your own sandwiches in here!"

The Brighton and Hove Albion Fans looked at each other, shrugged their shoulders and then exchanged sandwiches.

———•———

Why is it good to have a Brighton and Hove Albion Fan as a passenger?

Because you can park in the handicapped zone.

———•———

"If there are any idiots in the room, will they please stand up," said the Brighton and Hove Albion Fan giving a lecture.

After a long silence, one attendee rose to his feet.

"Now," asked the Brighton and Hove Albion Fan. "Why do you consider yourself an idiot?"

"Well, actually I don't," replied the attendee. "But I hate seeing you standing up here all by yourself."

What do UFOs and smart Brighton and Hove Albion Fans have in common?

You hear about them all the time but you never see one.

How can you tell if a Brighton and Hove Albion Fan made the chocolate chip cookies?

There are M&Ms shells on the floor.

A successful Brighton and Hove Albion Fan parked his brand new Porsche in front of the office to show it off to his colleagues. As he got out, a truck came along too close to the curb and completely tore off the driver's side.

The Brighton and Hove Albion Fan immediately called 911 and in less than 5 minutes the law arrived. Before the police officer could ask any questions, the Brighton and Hove Albion Fan started screaming about how his brand-new car would never be the same again.

After the Brighton and Hove Albion Fan had finished his rant, the police officer shook his head in disbelief.

"I can't believe how materialistic you Brighton and Hove Albion Fans are," he said. "You're so focused on your possessions you don't notice anything else."

"How can you say that?," asked the Brighton and Hove Albion Fan.

The police officer replied: "Haven't you noticed that your left arm is missing from your elbow down? It was torn off when the truck hit you."

The Brighton and Hove Albion Fan looked down in absolute horror and screamed: "Where's my Rolex?"

———•———

Then there was a female Brighton and Hove Albion Fan who went swimming off the coast of Hawaii because she heard they were man-eating sharks.

———•———

Did you hear about the Brighton and Hove Albion Fan who wore a glove on one hand?

The forecaster said: "Tomorrow may be hot, but on the other hand, it could be cold."

———•———

A Brighton and Hove Albion Fan was on vacation and was told about a great restaurant in town, but thought it was closed because the sign in the window said: "Home Cooking."

A Brighton and Hove Albion Fan went into a bar with burnt feet. The barman said: "How did you burn your feet?"

The Brighton and Hove Albion Fan said: "Cooking spaghetti."

"How on earth can you burn your feet cooking spaghetti?," asked the astonished barman.

"Easy," said the Brighton and Hove Albion Fan. "I just followed the instructions. They said: Pierce top of can and stand in boiling water."

A Brighton and Hove Albion Fan went to a baseball game with a friend, but got stuck in traffic and arrived after the fifth inning. When they arrived, the score was still zero-zero.

"Oh good," said the Brighton and Hove Albion Fan, we haven't missed anything.

What do you call 16 Brighton and Hove Albion Fans standing in a room around a beer keg?

A dope ring.

Did you hear about the two not-so-bright Brighton and Hove Albion Fans who tried to make money selling watermelons?

They bought a truckload of melons for $5.00 each, and sold them for $5.00 each.

At the end of the day they sold everything they had bought, but couldn't work out why they had exactly the same amount of money as when they started.

"This isn't working," said one Brighton and Hove Albion Fan. "We're not making any money. What are we going to do?"

The other Brighton and Hove Albion Fan replied: "I guess we're going to have to get a bigger truck."

What's does a Brighton and Hove Albion Fan make for dinner?

Reservations.

A Brighton and Hove Albion Fan ordered a pizza. "Do you want it cut into four or eight slices?," asked the pizza maker.

The Brighton and Hove Albion Fan replied: "Better make it four, I'm not very hungry."

———•———

A Brighton and Hove Albion Fan went to the doctor and asked how to have a better sex life. The doctor said: "Run five miles a day."

A week later the doctor called and said: "How is your sex life?"

The Brighton and Hove Albion Fan said: "I don't know, I'm 35 miles from home."

———•———

Did you hear about the Brighton and Hove Albion Fan who wore two jackets when he painted his house?

The instructions on the can said: "Put on two coats."

———•———

Why do Brighton and Hove Albion Fans laugh three times when they hear a joke?

Once when it is told, once when it is explained to them, and once when they understand it.

———•———

How do you make a Brighton and Hove Albion Fan's eyes light up?

Shine a flashlight in their ear.

———•———

Two Brighton and Hove Albion Fans rented a boat to go fishing in their local lake. Amazed at the number of fish they caught, they decided to come back the next day to try their luck again.

The first Brighton and Hove Albion Fan asked: "How will we find this spot again?"

The second Brighton and Hove Albion Fan takes a can of spray paint, paints an X on the bottom of the boat, and says: "We'll just look for this X tomorrow."

The first Brighton and Hove Albion Fan said: "You idiot! How do you know we'll get the same boat?"

———•———

Did you hear about the Buddhist Brighton and Hove Albion Fan who refused Novocaine during a root canal? The goal: transcend dental medication.

A priest was seated next to a Brighton and Hove Albion Fan on a flight to Texas. After the plane took off, the Brighton and Hove Albion Fan ordered a gin and tonic, which was brought and placed before him.

The flight attendant then asked the preacher if he wanted a drink.

Appalled, the preacher said: "I'd rather be tied up and taken advantage of by women of ill-repute, rather than let liquor touch my lips."

The Brighton and Hove Albion Fan then handed his drink back to the attendant and said: "Me too, I didn't know we had a choice."

During a visit to the doctor, a Brighton and Hove Albion Fan asks: "How do you determine whether a person should be put in an insane asylum?"

"The doctor said: "We fill up a bathtub and offer the person a teaspoon, cup and a bucket and ask them to empty the tub."

"I understand," said the Brighton and Hove Albion Fan. "A normal person would use the bucket because it's bigger than the spoon or the teacup."

"No," said the doctor. "A normal person would pull the plug. Do you want a bed near the window or the door?"

Two Brighton and Hove Albion Fans were adrift in a lifeboat. While rummaging through the boat's provisions the first Brighton and Hove Albion Fan found a rusty old lamp.

He rubs the lamp and a genie suddenly appears. "Thank you for freeing me," said the genie. "Due to the current economic situation and the cutbacks, I can only grant you one wish.

"That's OK," replied the first Brighton and Hove Albion Fan. "All I want you to do is turn the entire ocean into beer."

The genie clapped his hands with a deafening crash, and suddenly the entire sea became beer.

The genie disappeared, and only the gentle lapping of beer on the hull broke the stillness as the two Brighton and Hove Albion Fans considered their circumstances.

"Nice going," said the second Brighton and Hove Albion Fan. "Now we're going to have to pee in the boat."

———•———

A Brighton and Hove Albion Fan checked into a room at his hotel and asked the lady at the registration desk if the porn channel in his room was disabled.

"No, it's regular porn, you sick bastard," replied the desk clerk.

———•———

THE PERSONALIZED EDITION

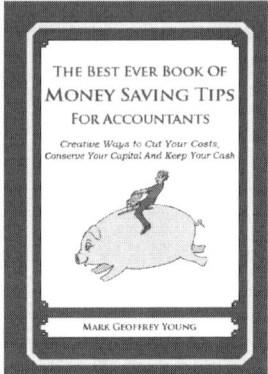

If you'd like to make this book your own, why not order a personalized copy for yourself or a friend. Simply go to www.dolyttle.com and order a copy of The Best Ever Book of YOUR NAME Jokes, The Best Ever Guide to Demotivation for YOUR NAME, or The Best Ever Book of Money Saving Tips for YOUR NAME.

We'll put your name and picture on the cover and throughout the book. Or, if you'd rather, simply order one of the many titles available.

At $19.95 per copy it's a great deal. Simply go to www. dolyttle.com.

ORDER! FORM

Dolyttle & Seamore
198 Garth Road Suite 2D
Scarsdale, NY 10583
212-496-8771 • info@dolyttle.com
(For faster service go to www.dolyttle.com)

Name

Address   Apt.

City   State   ZIP

Country

Email

Phone

Title: The Best Ever Book of _____Jokes

Friend's Name _____ _

If you don't have a friend, don't worry about it. We'll nominate somebody be your friend, at absolutely no additional cost. Each book is $19.95 plus $3.99 shipping for the first book and $2.00 for each additional copy. Call for pricing for large orders and corporate prices.

WWW.DOLYTTLE.COM

Occupations

OCCUPATIONS

Account Executive, Acccountant, Actor, Acupuncturist, Administrative Assistant, Administrator, Aide, Air Force, Air Traffic Controller, Ambulance Officer, Analyst, Anesthesiologist, Announcer, Antique Dealer, Architect, Army, Assistant, Astronomer, Athlete, Audiologist, Auditor, Author, Baker, Balloon Artist, Banker, Barber, Barista, Bartender, Beautician, Beekeeper, Benefit Manager, Bill Collector, Biologist, Bodybuilder, Book Seller, Bookkeeper, Bricklayer, Builder, Building Manager, Bus Driver, Business Owner, Butcher, Camera Operator, Camp Counselor, Camp Director, Candy Store Owner, Car Salesman, Caregiver, Carpenter, Carpet Layer, Carpet Salesperson, Cartographer, Chauffeur, Chef, Chemical Engineer, Chemist, Chiropractor, Cinematographer, Civil Engineer, Civil Servant, Claims Adjuster, Clerk, Clown, Coach, Coast Guard, Company Director, Compliance Officer, Computer Engineer, Computer Operator, Computer, Programmer, Conductor, Conference Producer, Congressman, Conservationist, Cook, Copy Editor Corrections Officer, Counselor, Courier Criminal, Cyclist, Dancer Data Entry Operator, Debt Collector, Deli Owner, Delivery Person, Dental Assistant, Dental Hygienist, Dental Technician, Dentist, Dermatologist, Designer, Detailer, Detective, Dispatcher, Doctor, Dog Walker, Doorman, Dressmaker, Driver, Drug Dealer, Dry Cleaner, Electrician, Engineer, Engraver, Entertainer, Entrepreneur, Environmental Engineer, Epidemiologist, Episcopalian, Executive, Exporter, Falcons' Fan, Farmer, Fire Fighter, Fireman, Fisherman, Fitness Instructor, Flight Attendant, Flight Engineer, Florist, Flower Seller, Food Technologist, Funeral Director, Furniture Maker, Furniture Salesperson, Garbage Collector, Gardener, Geologist, Golfer, Graphic Designer, Grave Digger, Grocer, Guard, Hairdresser, Handyman, Hardware Store, Owner, Historian, Horticulturist, Host, Hostess, Human Resource, Consultant, Human Resource, Manager, Importer, Industrial Engineer, Information Systems, Manager, Information Technology, Manager, Inspector, Instructor, Intelligence Officer, Interpreter, Janitor, Jeweler, Journalist, Judge, Laborer, Labourer, Landscaper, Law Clerk, Lawyer, Life Guard, Locksmith, Machinist, Magician, Mail Carrier, Mail Sorter, Mailman, Makeup Artist, Manager, Managing Director, Manicurist, Marines, Marriage Counselor, Mathematician, Mechanic, Medical Assistant, Medical Technician, Messenger, Meteorologist, Meter Reader, Midwife, Miner, Minister, Model, Musician, National Guard, Naturalist, Naturopath, Navy, Notary Public, Nuclear Engineer, Nuclear Physicist, Nurse, Nursing Aide, Obstetrician, Occupational Therapist, Optician, Orthodontist, Paralegal, Parking Inspector, Parole Officer, Party Planner, Payroll Clerk, Pediatric Oncologist, Pediatrician, Pharmacist, Pharmacy, Technician, Philosopher, Physical Therapist, Physician, Physician's Assistant, Physician's Assistant, Physicist, Physiotherapist, Pilot, Plumber, Podiatrist, Police, Political Scientist, Postal Carrier, Postal Worker, Postman, Postmaster, Potter, PR Executive, President, Priest, Printer, Prison Guard, Prison Officer, Probation Officer, Producer, Professor, Programmer, Projectionist, Proofreader, Prostitute, Psychiatric Nurse, Psychiatrist, Psychic, Psychologist, Public Servant, Purchasing Manager, Rabbi, Radiographer, Radiologist, Real Estate, Refrigeration Mechanic, Registrar, Repairman, Reporter, Roofer, Rubbish Collector, Sailor, Sales Manager Joke, Salesman, Salesperson, Scientist, Secretary, Security Guard Joke, Senator, Sheriff, Shoemaker, Shop Assistant, Sign Writer, Singer, Skin Care Specialist, Small Business Owner, Social Worker, Socialist, Sociologist, Sound Technician, Speech Therapist, Spy, Statistician, Student, Subeditor, Superintendent, Surfer, Surgeon, Surveillance Officer, Surveyor, Swimmer, Swimming Instructor, Tailor, Taxi Driver, Teacher, Teaching Assistant, Technician, Technologist, Technology Writer, Telemarketer, Therapist, Ticket Collector, Tire Dealer, Tire Technician, Title Examiner, Tour Guide, Trainer, Travel Agent, Truck Driver, Tutor, Tyre Dealer, Tyre Technician, Umpire, Undertaker, Underwriter, Upholsterer, Urban Planner, Urologist, Usher, Veterinarian, Waiter, Waitress, Web Designer, Welder, Window Washer, Zookeeper, Zoologist

NATIONALITIES

Afghan, Albanian, Algerian, American, Andorran, Angolan, Anguillan, Antiguan, Argentinean, Armenian, Australian, Austrian, Azerbaijani, Bahamian, Bahraini, Bangladeshi, Barbadian, Batswana, Belarusian, Belgian, Belizean, Beninese, Bermudian, Bhutanese, Bolivian, Bosnian, Brazillian, British, Bruneian, Bulgarian, Burkinabe, Burmese, Burundian, Cambodian, Cameroonian, Canadian, Cape Verdian, Caymanian, Central African, Chadian, Chilean, Chinese, Christmas Islander, Cocos Islander, Colombian, Comoran, Congolese, Costa Rican, Croat, Cuban, Cypriot, Czech, Danish, Djibouti, Dominica, Dutch, East Timorese, Ecuadorean, Egyptian, Emirati, English, Equatoguinean, Eritrean, Estonian, Ethiopian, Falkland Islander, Fijian, Filipino, Finnish, French, Gabonese, Gambian, Georgian, German, Ghanaian, Gibraltarian, Greek, Greenlander, Grenadian, Guadeloupian, Guatemalan, Guianese, Guinea-Bissauan, Guinean, Guyanese, Haitian, Herzegovinian, Honduran, Hungarian, Icelandic, Indian, Indonesian, Iraqi, Irish, Israeli, Italian, Jamaican, Japanese, Jordanian, Kazakhstani, Kenyan, Kiribati, Kittian, Korean, Kuwaiti, Kyrgyzstani, Laotian, Latvian, Lebanese, Liberian, Libyan, Liechtensteiner, Lithuanian, Luxembourger, Macedonian, Madagascan, Mahorais, Malagasy, Malawian, Malaysian, Maldivian, Malian, Maltese, Marshallese, Martinican, Mauritanian, Mauritian, Mexican, Micronesian, Moldovan, Monacan, Mongolian, Montenegrin, Montserratian, Moroccan, Mozambican, Myanmarese, Namibian, Nauruan, Nepalese, Netherlander, Nevisian, New Zealand, New Zealander, Nicaraguan, Niger, Nigerian, Nigerien, Norwegian, Omani, Pakistani, Palauan, Palestinian, Panamanian, Papua, New Guinean, Paraguayan, Peruvian, Polish, Portuguese, Puerto Rican, Qatari, Reunionese, Romanian, Russian, Rwandan, Saint Helenian, Saint Lucian, Saint Vincentian, Salvadoran, Sammarinese, Sao Tomean, Saudi Arabian, Scottish, Senegalese, Serbian, Seychellois, Sierra Leonean, Singaporean, Slovakian, Slovene, Solomon Islander, Somali, Somalian, South African, Spaniard, Spanish, Sri Lankan, Sudan, Sudanese, Surinamer, Swazi, Swedish, Swiss, Syrian, Taiwanese, Tajik, Tanzanian, Thai, Tobagonian, Togolese, Tongan, Trinidadian, Tunisian, Turkish, Turkmen, Tuvaluan, Ugandan, Ukrainian, Uruguayan, Uzbekistani, Vanuatu, Venezuelan, Vietnamese, Virgin Islander, Welsh, Yemeni, Zambian, Zimbabwean and others

SPORTS

Adventure, Archery, Badminton, Athlete, Baseball, Basketball, Bodybuilder, Bowling, Boxing, Canoeist, Coach, Cricket, Cyclist, Dancer, Diving, Fencing, Fisherman, Fitness Instructor Football, Golfer, Gymnast, Handball, Hiking, Hockey, Horse Riding, Hunting, Jockey, Kayaker, Mountaineer, Orienteering, Pilot, Ping Pong, Polo, Racing, Racquetball, Referee, Rower, Rugby, Runner, Sailor, Skier, Shooter, Soccer Softball, Squash, Surfer, Swimmer, Swimming Instructor, Table Tennis, Trainer, Tramping, Umpire, Volleyball, Weightlifter, Wrestling

Baseball

Angels, Astros, Athletics, Blue Jays, Braves, Brewers, Cardinals, Cubs, Diamondbacks, Dodgers, Giants, Indians, Mariners, Marlins, Mets, Nationals, Orioles, Padres, Phillies, Pirates, Rangers, Rays, Red Sox, Reds, Rockies, Royals, Tigers, Twins, White Sox, Yankees

Baseball

76ers, Blazers, Bobcats, Bucks, Bulls, Cavaliers, Celtics, Clippers, Grizzlies, Hawks, Heat, Hornets, Jazz, Kings, Knicks, Lakers, Magic, Mavericks, Nets, Nuggets, Pacers, Pistons, Raptors, Rockets, Spurs, Suns, Thunder, Timberwolves, Warriors, Wizards

American Football

Football, Soccer, 49ers, Bears, Bengals, Bills, Broncos, Browns, Buccaneers, Cardinals, Chargers, Chiefs, Colts, Cowboys, Dolphins, Eagles, Falcons, Giants, Jaguars, Jets, Lions, Packers, Panthers,

Patriots, Raiders, Rams, Ravens, Redskins, Saints, Seahawks, Steelers, Texans, Titans, Vikings

English Football / English Soccer
Football, Soccer, Arsenal, Aston Villa, Chelsea, Everton, Fulham, Liverpool, Manchester City, Manchester United, Newcastle United, Norwich City, Queens Park, Rangers, Reading, Southampton, Stoke City, Sunderland, Swansea City, Tottenham Hotspur, West Bromwich, Albion, West Ham United, Wigan Athletic

SEXUAL
Gay, Homosexual, Lesbian, Masturbator, Nudist, Pervert, Prostitute, Transsexual, Wanker

MEDICAL
Acupuncturist, Ambulance Officer, Anesthesiologist Biologist, Chemist, Chiropractor, Counselor, Dental Assistant, Dental Hygienist, Dental Technician, Dermatologist, Doctor, Naturopath, Nurse, Nursing Aide, Obstetrician, Occupational Therapist, Optician, Orthodontist, Pediatric Oncologist, Pediatrician, Pharmacist, Pharmacy, Technician, Physician, Physician's Assistant Joke, Physical Therapist, Podiatrist, Physiotherapist, Psychiatric Nurse, Psychologist, Psychiatrist, Radiologist, Radiographer, Surgeon, Therapist, Undertaker, Urologist, Veterinarian

GENERAL
Blind, Blond, Boy Scout, Brunette, Cat Lover, Conservationist, Criminal, Dog Lover, Drug Dealer, Essex Girl, Girl Scout, Pilot, Redhead, Redneck, Vegan, Vegetarian

CREATIVE
Actor, Artist, Author, Balloon Artist, Cinematographer, Clown, Conductor, Dancer, Designer, Dressmaker, Entertainer, Graphic Designer, Hat Maker, Pilot, Singer, Woodworker, Writer

RELIGION
Atheist, Baptist, Born Again, Buddhist, Catholic, Christian, Episcopalian, Jehovah's Witness, Jewish, Mormon, Muslim, Pagan, Protestant, Scientologist, Witch, Unitarian

POLITICAL
Barack Obama, Christian Democrat, Communist, Congressman, Conservative, Criminal, Democrat, Glenn Beck, Independent, Labour, Liberal, Libertarian, Michael Bloomberg, Michele Bachmann, Mitt Romney, Newt Gingrich, Non-Voter, Republican, Senator, Social Democrat, Socialist, Tea Party

Printed in Great Britain
by Amazon